American Christmas

ESPECIALLY FOR GEORGE AND VIRGINIA —

American Christmas

by JIM HARRISON

LONGSTREET PRESS, INC.
Atlanta, Georgia

Published by
LONGSTREET PRESS, INC.
A subsidiary of Cox Newspapers,
A division of Cox Enterprises, Inc.
2140 Newmarket Parkway
Suite 118
Marietta, GA 30067

Printed in the United States of America

Color Separations and film preparation by Holland Graphics, Inc.
Mableton, Georgia

1st printing 1994

Library of Congress Catalog Card Number: 94-77586

ISBN 1-56352-174-1

Jacket design by Laura McDonald

Book design by Jill Dible

Special thanks to John Burks.

For information regarding original artwork, write:
Jim Harrison
1 S. Main St.
Denmark, SC 29042

Contents

JimHarrison

Prologue

I too, dream of a white Christmas. It would be oh so nice riding through a winter wonderland in a one-horse open sleigh with bells ringing and children singing. Perhaps every American yearns to experience Christmas-card Christmases as portrayed by the tranquil Currier & Ives scenes of years past.

After all, the very message of the One whose birthday we celebrate is of serenity, peace, brotherhood, and love of our fellow man. Christmas should be a joyous season with time for family, friends, and the old home place and a rallying period for fond memories of Christmases past.

A celebration which, originally, was centered entirely around hope for the future, Christmas is now balanced with a tugging from behind that constantly pleads for us to turn around and look to the past. Many of our adult habits and activities are influenced by traditions tied to how we grew up, where we lived, and the things we were taught.

Within our lifetimes we see many changes, but the Christmas customs we learned as youth build upon themselves. By way of the hand-me-down process, customs become basic to our grown-up lives just as they will to the lives of our children and their children after them.

True, the passing of years well may dim the twinkle in our eyes and memories may not leap forward quite so quickly, but our childhood days do, indeed, mold and shape the way we do things forever. And so it is, Christmas is a time for doing it the old way.

When I was growing up in Denmark, South Carolina, I remember that every year atop our tree sat a well-worn, homemade, wooden angel which once belonged to my mother's mother. From such a lofty position, the white-robed angel watched over at least a quarter century of happy Christmases as the Harrison boys discovered Santa Claus and ripped open presents. The angel is now among the most prized possessions that came to me from my mother.

Many family heirloom lists include similar Christmas decorations which have served more than one generation and have passed from parents to children. Even at this most spiritual time of the year we cannot avoid our passion for nostalgia, and the season brings out an abundance of reissued collectibles from the past. Treasured Christmas tins and ornaments and even antique images of Santa, himself, work their way into the season.

We Americans are among the few people who have hybrid traditions peculiar solely to us. Our Christmas ways, as with all our other ways, are a hodgepodge of traditions belonging to the millions of European immigrants who arrived in New York City. They brought with them from across the seas hundreds of ancient customs that were poured into the melting pot. Through the years, this variety has been diffused and blended into today's holiday celebration. Some of the Old World ways have been lost and forgotten, but many have endured; combined with New World modifications, they make for a seasonal experience that is as American as pumpkin pie.

No other holiday is so rich in spirit, nostalgia, and tradition, yet the stresses of December 25 come dangerously close to overshadowing the real meaning. Always, there has been a battle between the sacred and the secular. And so today, in our highly materialistic society, it is frightening, but not surprising, to find a decline in the spiritual essence that was so central to our American forebears' celebration.

By no means is Christmas all good for all people. "I'll be glad when it's over," or, "I'm thankful that it just comes once a year," expresses the prevalent weariness that commercialization has caused.

For such people, the season of happiness, merrymaking, and rejoicing has become a time of want, discontentment, and disappointment. Unfortunately, the pressures of modern times have changed the most loved day of the year to a time of dread. But still, many people want to experience the mystery and spirit of that first Christmas. They take time to pause, reflect, and rejoice in the birth of Christ; they marvel over the strange miracle that happened some two thousand years ago halfway around the world. In those hearts and those souls the true meaning of Christmas can be found.

Despite all our shortcomings and the weaknesses of human nature, Christmastime well may be Americans' finest hour. It is then that we come closest to being what we should be. We give more thought to other people during the Christmas season than at any other time of the year.

Benevolence, generosity, and kindness lead us on that day. Expressions of love and goodwill

are vital aspects of the occasion. Good deeds represent the original spirit of the holy day and give rise to the hope that commercial exploitation will not overtake us.

As America has grown, so has Christmas and so have social needs. Some well-organized groups are now particularly active.

Hardly a city street corner in the nation is without the kettles and bell ringers of the Salvation Army. Volunteers from all walks of life contribute their time, wear Santa Claus suits, and visit hospitals. Institutions, newspapers, and fraternal organizations collect millions of dollars to aid the poor.

Police officers and firemen gather toys. Coins are generously dropped into the cups of the blind, the lame, and the homeless. This is the American way.

For centuries, Christians around the world have told and retold the simple story of the baby born in Bethlehem. The facts of the event remain literally unchanged after two thousand years, but the history of the ways men and women have shown their joy over the birth is quite varied and oftentimes conflicting.

From every corner of the world, a variety of rituals, ceremonies, music, feasting, and pageantry have evolved into the reverence and gaiety we now enjoy. Our American heritage has been to combine the old ways into the new. I have long been curious about the unusual medley of our customs: What are their origins? How have they become part of our American Christmas? I sought out the answers to these questions, and the fruits of my research make up this book. To know and understand our traditions' significance, I believe, is to enjoy them to their fullest. ∎

American Christmas

Joseph, the respected, middle-aged carpenter of Nazareth, had dreamed only of a simple life with his beautiful, young, espoused wife, Mary. The two were content with their appointed lot in life, and their riches were not to be of material things but of the promises made by God to the people of Israel.

Obscurity was welcomed, and both agreed the opulence of the world could pass them by without giving them an envious thought.

Joseph was a maker of fine furniture and loved his trade, handed down to him by his father and his father's father before him. The quiet, peaceful Nazarethian days were spent in his carpentry shop among fresh shavings from the tasks at hand. Always, the fragrance of well-seasoned lumber filled the air.

Mary, too, joyfully went about her routine chores of baking, sewing, cleaning, washing, and fetching jugs of water. As with the masculine trades, these skills were passed from mother to daughter. Little did either know of the holy events awaiting them.

The biblical story of the birth of Christ is presented briefly, with modest description, in only a few verses in the gospels of Saint Matthew and Saint Luke. And as it is told, Mary found that she was great with child before she and Joseph had been together. The expectant mother had no credible explanation for her pregnancy, but she made a strong vow that she had known no one. For a man of Nazareth in those times, such circumstances were very difficult to accept.

Bewildered, uncertain, and brokenhearted, Joseph considered ending the engagement to avoid any further embarrassment to himself, to her, or to the child. As he wondered what he must do, an angel of the Lord appeared in a dream and explained that the child was the Son of God, and would one day save the people of Israel from their sins. Joseph did not understand this, but he was a believing man and accepted without question the angel's message. Strengthened with renewed love for Mary and for life, he resumed his carpentry business so he could provide for her and her eminent Child.

As he worked and as Mary's time was passing, a startling decree went out from the emperor of Rome, Caesar Augustus, that all of the Roman world must be enrolled for the payment of a new tax. Each man must go to his ancestral home and personally place his name by family and tribe on the tax list, according to Jewish law.

Daring not to disobey the emperor's command, Joseph prepared for the hard trip. He purchased a donkey to carry Mary over the rough parts of the 100-mile journey, and they packed rations to sustain them along the way.

It was the third week in December when Joseph and Mary joined with others of the family of David who also were traveling to Bethlehem. The southern route from Nazareth passed through the country of Samaria and over the peaceful hills of Judea into Jerusalem. Travelers from elsewhere in the empire were arriving daily in the small city of Bethlehem for the same purpose. Toward nightfall on December 24, a weary Joseph and Mary slowly made their way over the last rugged hill into David's city and found the courtyard of the village inn swarming with people and animals in noisy confusion. Usually by early afternoon, the inn was filled to capacity. Not a vacant spot was available anywhere, even to place a mat for sleeping. The night winds were already sharp and cold as they came across the rolling hills of Moab. A light rain added to the couple's discomfort. The only possibility for shelter in Bethlehem was behind the inn in the limestone cave that served as a stable for the animals.

It was there on this holy night that Joseph, using his goat hair cloak, prepared a mat on the fresh straw for the expectant Mary. And it was there that her time did come, and she brought forth the Baby Jesus. With no crib to cradle the Infant, Mary wrapped the young Messiah in soft swaddling clothes and laid Him in the manger. Only scattered starlight penetrated the blackness of the cave, and there was no fire to warm them.

According to tradition, at that time a strange calm fell over Bethlehem, and a bright star appeared directly over the stable. No trumpets sounded in the sleeping town, and no messengers raced through the streets announcing the arrival of the tiny Baby. Babies were born every day, after all, but this Baby and this event would change the world. The mother who had given birth was a virgin, and the Child was the Son of God.

That night outside Bethlehem of Judea, shepherds were watching their flock. They noticed the strange, bright light, and they were frightened as an angel of the Lord appeared to them and announced the heavenly news. "Behold, I bring you good tidings of great joy, which shall be to all people, for unto you is born this day in the City of David a Savior which is Christ the Lord." The awestruck shepherds listened in great wonder to how Christ was born in a Bethlehem manager, and they immediately wanted to see Him. With all haste they left their flock and went to the lowly cave behind the inn. Once inside, the shepherds fell to their knees and worshiped the holy Infant. This was the very first Christmas, almost two thousand years ago.

❋ ❋ ❋

The accurate date of the momentous birth will always remain unknown, clouded with mystery and uncertainty. For more than three hundred years His birthday was celebrated at various times of the year. The Eastern world recognized His birth in the spring, but at the same time Christians of the Western world honored Him in either November or December. The lack of written records allowed the uncertainty to continue for many years before a date was finally determined. Scholars argued that it could not have been in December, for at that time of the year the winter rains were strong in Palestine and roads were impassable. The shepherds and their flock would not have been on the hillside.

In 337 A.D., in an attempt to clear up the confusion, the Pope assigned to Cyril, the Bishop of Jerusalem, the task of determining a date for all the world to recognize as Christmas. It was not an easy matter to reconcile and required some years of study and negotiation. In 354 A.D., Bishop Liberius of Rome announced that December 25 would be the official date for Christmas.

Christians have universally agreed that the magnitude of the event is far greater than the significance of the exact date, and the birth of Christ has had a permanent effect on how the world has marked time since that night in tiny Bethlehem twenty centuries ago.

In the early part of the sixth century, Dionysus Exiguous eliminated the founding of Rome as the basal point of the calendar and introduced the Latin phrase *Anno Domini*, "in the year of our Lord," behind the numeral. Thus 1 A.D., the year of the Nativity, marks the beginning of modern time.

The study of Christmas is complex from any perspective. The setting of the December date and many of the traditional aspects of the celebration, surprisingly, have origins totally separated from the birth of Christ. Some even predate the event.

December 21, the time of the winter solstice, has always been a time of midwinter rejoicing. Ancient people believed that the sun was the source and giver of all life. It, therefore, was the center of many pagan religions. The beginning of the lengthening of days was viewed as the promise,

once again, of a new season. People from every civilization have always had a tendency to praise this reassurance with expressions of gladness, merriment, and various forms of worship.

For centuries, historians have noted that various midwinter festivals took place among many peoples, including the Scandinavians, Persians, Phoenicians, and Egyptians. In Rome, one such ritual, the Saturnalia or feast of Saturn, occurred at the time of the winter solstice and was the greatest event on the Roman calendar. During the celebration no one did work in the city, and all social distinctions were laid aside. Masters and slaves feasted one with another; they decorated their homes with evergreens and flowers. The poor and the beggars were welcomed at the palace door, and everyone shared gift giving, singing, dancing, and friendship.

In their effort to determine an exact date for Christ's birth, the early church leaders saw advantages of combining the estab-

lished festivals of midwinter with the commemoration of the Savior's birthday. The Roman Saturnalia focused on the return of the light from the sun, and Jesus Christ had brought the light of truth into the world.

For many years, the Christian rituals took place only inside the churches while the activities outside the church followed the pagan ways of the Romans. The old practices came not just from the Romans but also from other civilizations that acknowledged the winter solstice. So strong were both the influence of the old pagan customs and the indifference to the true Christian significance of the holiday that it took centuries for the real meaning of Christ's birth to reach the people. Even more difficult for the church was the task of convincing its worshippers that Christmas was more than just a festival; it should be a part of every home and every heart—a conscious expression of faith—throughout the Christian world.

Following closely the ways people celebrated Saturnalia, the early Christmas seasons were boisterous and lively. People sang carols and were accompanied by dancing, guitars, violins, tambourines, and organs. As Christianity replaced paganism, Christians adopted many of the old ways as part of their religious celebration.

During its nearly 2,000-year history, Christmas has passed through good times and bad. The peasants of rural Europe were hardworking laborers who toiled from sunrise to sunset for a meager living. They had few pleasures in life, so holidays were looked forward to with eager anticipation. At yuletide, the workers' problems could be left in the fields for the moment. They could forget about low wages and high taxes and enjoy themselves.

It was out of these conditions that a strange stepchild of Christmas, the practice called the Lord of Misrule, grew. This seemingly innocent custom became popular quite by accident. Prevailing for more than a century, the rule established the appointing of a Boy Bishop to preside over church services on Christmas Day. Boy Bishops were carefully selected based upon good character. To be chosen was a high honor, and the favored boy likewise appointed officers who were of the highest disposition.

With the passing of years, however, the custom changed for the worse. In the sixteenth-century England of Elizabeth I, the Boy Bishop become a lawless tyrant who allowed the recognition of Christmas to degenerate into nothing more than an unruly, rowdy party. People began calling him the Lord of Misrule, and his aides were the Fool and the Jester. It was this trio who planned and ruled over the Christmas carnival. The boisterous merrymakers forgot the true meaning of Christmas and, in fact, desecrated the day.

These circumstances surrounded the yuletide season in England when Puritanism emerged. A no-nonsense, stern, and pious sect, the Puritans looked upon this wild manner of observing Christmas with horror. Their influence in English government became sufficiently strong, in 1643, to abolish Christmas from the calendar altogether. And so it was in the early American colonies that the same attitude among the Puritans placed restraints on Christmas observances. ■

It is believed that on Christmas Day in 1492 the thoughts of Admiral Christopher Columbus were on the magnificent event that occurred in Bethlehem some fifteen hundred years earlier. The Spanish explorer was leading an expedition in the West Indies when his flag ship, the *Santa Maria*, ran aground and began to leak. The logbook entry of the day describes the activities of the crew, who, with the help of the local Indians, spent December 25 salvaging the stranded vessel's cargo. More than likely, the men were much too busy to stop and celebrate. The following day, however, the sailors and the natives feasted together. The Indians presented Columbus with gifts of gems, silver, and gold. The sailors, in turn, demonstrated for their hosts the magic of firearms and gun powder. This was the first American Christmas. In honor of the occasion, the new colony was named La Navidad, the Spanish word for the holiday.

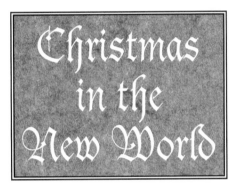

Christmas in the New World

Little is documented about the early Portuguese and Spanish who explored parts of the New World in the fifteenth and sixteenth centuries. Both countries were on the descending slope of their high civilizations, and their attempts to gain new territories were limited. Spain and Portugal did make some attempts at settlements in the South and the Southwest. It would therefore be reasonable to assume that some other Christmas celebrations occurred during that time.

In the 1500s, the British were a proud and aggressive people with a strong desire to add new territories to their empire. England's maritime might was unquestioned, and it became the dominant country in colonizing and attempting to settle the New World. The first permanent English settlement, however, was not until 1607, at Jamestown, Virginia.

The first documented English Christmas in America was not a happy one. More than half of the men of Jamestown had died of hunger. Only forty survivors remained, and they gathered on that cold bleak day in a small wooden chapel to hear the biblical account of the birth of Christ. There were no women to prepare a feast. The leader of the colony, Captain John Smith, was a prisoner of the Indians. Frightened, hungry, and cold, the settlers were very unsure of their future.

By the next Christmas in Jamestown, Pocahontas had saved Captain Smith's life and the Indians had become more helpful and friendly to the settlers. The men spent the second yuletide in an Indian village feasting on oysters, fish, wild turkey, and bread. Smith's December 25, 1608, diary entry read, "An Englishman where ever he is must celebrate Christmas with feasting and merriment." As the Virginia settlement grew and eventually women immigrated, the colonists celebrated Christmas in the New World just as they had observed the occasion in England. For them, it was both a sacred holy day and a fun-loving holiday.

By contrast, the Pilgrims spent December 25 of 1620, their first day at Plymouth Rock, working hard building a community storehouse. Only the sick, who remained aboard the anchored *Mayflower*, were excused from the hard labor. This strict Puritanical group had banned the gaiety of Christmas in England and had brought with them to the New World the same restrictions. For them, Christmas was entirely a religious matter and no signs of merriment out of the ordinary were allowed. They outlawed any expression of Christmas greetings. None of the traditional Christmas foods were allowed. Even the schools stayed open. Governor William Bradford admonished those few who felt like feasting rather than working on Christmas Day in 1621.

Bradford is often accused of having been totally anti-Christmas, but it must be remembered that the men and women of the Massachusetts Bay Colony were strict Puritans who had come west to purify the Church of England. Ironically, though they were not allowed to exchange gifts on Christmas Day, they were expected to extend help to their less fortunate neighbors at any time. The harsh environment did not allow

for many extras, but the Puritans were sharing people who inwardly yearned for the joy of yuletide giving.

The Puritan "no festivals laws" were eventually abolished in 1681, but the old attitudes lingered for years among the strict sect. It was not until 1856 that Christmas was recognized as a legal holiday in Massachusetts.

Elsewhere in the American colonies, Christmas was a time of good cheer, happiness, and merriment. Four years after the Pilgrims landed at Plymouth Rock, an expedition of the Dutch East India Company arrived in New York Harbor. On Christmas Day of 1624, the Dutch went ashore on what is now Manhattan and celebrated by feasting and dancing with the Manhattan Indians. The colonists that followed from Holland brought with them additional lively Christmas traditions.

Even though various customs

differed, immigrants from other countries joined the Dutch in keeping the American Christmas celebration joyous and festive. As the flow of immigrants increased and the population spread, new yuletide customs appeared all over the country.

The eighteenth century in the colonies was filled with political unrest. A strong desire for freedom prevailed in the hearts of all Americans. The turmoil climaxed when the Americans stated their right to govern themselves on July 4, 1776, with the signing of the Declaration of Independence. After winning their freedom in the Revolutionary War, the colonies again were in a constant struggle to rule themselves. The Constitution replaced the inefficient Articles of the Confederation, but by no means did all the people favor the new stronger central government. There was continued dissention and disagreement.

JIM HARRISON

Throughout this trying period, however, Christmas was well established as a time to put aside differences and enjoy merrymaking, relaxing, and worshiping. During the first year of his tenure as the first president of the United States, George Washington traveled to New York City to spend Christmas worshiping at St. Paul's Church. In following years, he returned to Mount Vernon for family gatherings, feasting, celebrating, and gift giving.

For the most part, the Methodist and Baptist churches took the lead in providing structured, sacred celebrations. They had programs devoted both to the Nativity story and to traditional religious music.

Most of the rural people in the young nation were struggling for simple economic survival. Out of

necessity, family celebrations in the home remained simple without many luxuries. Christmas in the early 1800s was good food shared with loved ones and friends.

By 1860, Christmas celebrations with feasting, gift giving, firecrackers, decorated trees, and Santa Claus were common to all of America. Even in the old Puritan stronghold in New England, the joyous spirit of the season prevailed and merriment and decorations filled the homes. Everywhere, city streets were lined with garlands, bell ringers, and strolling carolers.

The onslaught of the Civil War certainly had its impact on the celebration of Christmas, especially in the Confederate States of the South. In 1860, Southern men were far away on the battlefields while back at home food and other goods were scarce. Women were able only to make small gifts for their children, and, if lucky, somehow manage fruit and candy for the stockings.

With the end of the Civil War in 1865, yuletide observations were renewed in an even more festive and abundant atmosphere. By the 1890s, at the peak of the Victorian age, the year-end ritual was shaping into a true American tradition with its own unique character.

America was changing rapidly as it entered the twentieth century. Transportation and communication had dramatically improved, and the Industrial Revolution was well underway. The Victorian Christmas was quickly giving way to a more modern Christmas. Communities were gathering around giant public trees, and colored electric light bulbs were finding their way onto the branches. While public trees got bigger and bigger, ones for the home were scaling down, and even tabletop trees were in use.

Greeting cards were undergoing continuous change, too. Postcard greetings gave way to folded cards slipped into envelopes. The postal service, overwhelmed with the additional volume of mail, urged the public to mail early. Business offices were as elaborately decorated as city streets and public schools. Santa became a fat, jolly figure who received letters at every post office.

Today, America celebrates longer and with more enthusiasm than do any of the Old World countries, but the real reason for this once-a-year event is not forgotten. Either an angel or a star sit atop every tree, and Nativity scenes portraying Christ's birth adorn some spot in many homes. Individually, and as a nation, Americans, like no other people of the twentieth century, observe the true meaning of Christmas with charitable deeds, generosity, and good will toward all people. ■

Ancient primitive cultures looked upon evergreen plants and trees as being endowed with certain mystical powers that enabled the flora to remain alive during the coldest of winter months.

Green leaves and the bearing of cones and berries at the bleakest time of the year were signs of life and fertility and were a visual

promise of spring. Further, it was believed that the evergreen's thick, rough bark was a winter hiding place for certain friendly spirits during the winter months. So it followed in logical thought that taking trees or pieces of greenery indoors would encourage the friendly fairies to follow.

Even in prehistoric times people regularly took greenery inside during the winter months to protect their homes. During the Middle Ages, however, the evergreen assumed a different role.

The tradition of the Christmas tree has its roots in the fourteenth and fifteenth centuries. It came from the miracle plays that churches presented on December 24. Few people at that time could read or possessed a personal Bible, and these performances dramatized stories from the Scriptures as a way of teaching the congregation. At one time, December 24 appeared on the early church calendar as Adam and Eve's Day and was an occasion to dramatize the events that took place in the Garden of Eden. The play included scenes of Adam carrying a "Paradise Tree." Usually, the tree was the only prop in the play. Since the apple tree had bare branches in winter, an evergreen, decorated with apples, was substituted. By the seventeenth century, the apple-hung evergreen was no longer considered the "tree of temptation." It became the traditional Christmas tree. And to this day, a green tree adorned with apples is associated with Christmas. As late as the latter part of the nineteenth century in northern Germany, however, Christmas tree decorations included small figurines of Adam and Eve and a snake.

Most people associate the first Christmas trees with Germany because that country was the first to make the tree central in the celebration. It is believed that as Martin Luther, who founded the Lutheran church, was walking home through the woods from a church service a few nights before Christmas thinking of Jesus and His birth, he noticed how the bright stars in the sky seemed to be twinkling on the branches of the trees. Seizing the idea of decorating a tree to make it

sparkle, he cut a fir tree when he reached home, took it inside the house, attached candles to the branches, and lit them. His children gathered around and agreed that the effect did resemble the glittering of stars. From that time forward, people have placed lights on Christmas trees.

Records indicate that toward the mid-1800s there were trees of yuletide in England. The Royal Family at Windsor Castle made the custom popular. Queen Victoria's husband, Prince Albert, was a native of the German province, Saxe-Coburg, where the tree was an important feature of Christmas. In 1840, when Victoria and Albert's first son was born, a fir tree was brought into the royal parlor and trimmed with tapers, pretty baubles, and an angel at the top. The English people loved it.

Even though well accepted as a part of Christmas, the tree is not a universal custom in England. This is probably due to the lack of an inexpensive supply of evergreens. In some places, a living Christmas tree is preferred. A live tree is purchased, planted in a tub, and kept damp through the holiday season. It is later replanted outside and remembered as the tree of a specific year.

The Christmas tree came to America from Germany. On Christmas Day 1747, the members of the German Moravian settlement at Bethlehem, Pennsylvania, decorated for their children the first known Christmas trees in America. These were not actual trees, but were wooden pyramids covered with evergreen boughs.

It was two German teachers in America who helped further expand the Christmas tree custom. Charles Follen, a professor in Cambridge, Massachusetts, remembered that as a youngster growing up in Germany his parents always had a decorated tree. He wanted to pro-

vide the same seasonal atmosphere for his young son. In 1832, and every year thereafter, his home displayed a tree for his children and their friends to enjoy.

Charles Minnegerode came from Germany to teach in Williamsburg, Virginia. In 1842, he trimmed an evergreen for his schoolchildren, showing them how to paint nuts to hang on the limbs. The children also draped popcorn strings over the branches and wired candles in place. A handmade star was placed at the top of the tree.

Because early Christmas trees in America were a novelty and always drew attention, some smart-thinking fund-raisers came up with the idea of displaying a Christmas tree and charging a fee to see it. The Dorcas Society of York, Pennsylvania, advertised such an event, and the ladies collected six and a half cents to help clothe local widows and orphans.

Not every German family in

America had a Christmas tree during the first half of the nineteenth century, because, even in Germany, the custom was still spreading and had not yet become universal. As an American practice, Christmas trees did not catch on quickly, but all records do credit the Germans with having brought the tree to this country and with promoting the idea.

By 1850, some of the frontier town dwellers knew about the spreading custom. A variety of trees was abundant on the frontiers so that when conifers were rare, other types of trees simply were substituted. On the plains, sage or cedar brush was used, while coastal Texans decorated the sawed-off limbs of live oaks.

The first Christmas tree to appear in an American church caused quite an uprising. In 1851, a thirty-two-year-old German immigrant, Reverend Henry Schwan, placed a tree in his Cleveland sanctuary.

This had been a normal tradition in his native Hanover, but some disgruntled church members called it a throwback to pagan customs. Influenced by this resistance, Reverend Schwan decided against having a tree the next year.

Another Cleveland minister, Edwin Canfield, settled the issue by sending a tree over from his church to Schwan's. The displaying of trees in churches and Sunday schools quickly spread to other congregations in Ohio. Children who saw or helped decorate the pretty trees in their churches pressured their parents to have trees in their homes.

In 1856, President Franklin Pierce drew national attention by erecting the first White House Christmas tree. He invited hundreds of Sunday school children to come play and sing Christmas songs around the tree. News spread of the event to every corner of every state.

The decorated tree became a fashionable part of America's Victorian Christmas celebration. Trees were especially popular along the Atlantic seaboard and in San Francisco. Families carefully selected ceiling-tall trees. As is the practice today, the tree was placed in a stand on the floor rather than on a table. Parents usually decorated the tree on Christmas Eve after the children had gone to bed. Many youngsters were led to believe that Santa Claus brought the tree as well as the gifts.

Most early trees were decorated entirely with simple homemade gingerbread men, nuts painted different colors, candy canes, cookies, pine cones, dried seed pods, and strings of popcorn or cranberries. Small, yellow "ladies apples" were a widely used decoration, as were doughnuts, strings of dried apple slices, paper flowers, paper mottoes, and white sugar animals. The candles attached to the drying-out foliage posed a constant threat of fire, so buckets of water were stationed near every tree. A wet sponge on a long stick also was available to put out small blazes on a moment's notice.

When many Europeans immigrated to America, among the family possessions they brought were treasured glass Christmas tree ornaments. Not until 1870 were commercial decorations sold in America, and these were icicles and heavy glass balls imported from Germany. At first the glass ornaments were sold only in the German communities, but by the early 1880s many toy and variety stores enjoyed a brisk Christmas tree ornament business.

One night in 1895 a New England telephone worker named Ralph E. Morris watched the small, signal bulbs light up on a telephone switchboard and got the idea of placing electrically lit, colored lights on trees. He wired together a set of lights and strung them on his tree. With the invention of tree lights and the introduction of glass ornaments, a whole new industry was born. Very rapidly, Americans who could afford them shifted away from homemade decorations to the more popular "store bought" kind.

As the population in America increased, so did the year-end demand for Christmas trees. City folks could not go easily to the forest and cut a tree; they had to rely on others who brought trees to town. Farmers, with an eye for business, began bundling up trees and taking them to city produce markets.

The increasing demand for firs fast depleted a once abundant supply because individual farmers failed to replant what they had cut. But the idea of growing trees commercially caught on, and Christmas tree farms became quite profitable. Scotch pines and Dou-

glas firs became popular varieties.

To those parts of the country where evergreens were not available, growers shipped in quantities by train. For the trees, as with everything else, modern technology interfered with the old way of doing things. The master of mail-order marketing, Sears & Roebuck offered for sale the first artificial trees. With fifty-five limbs, the trees sold for one dollar. And today, for those desiring convenience and safety, the artificial tree is still the answer.

But the true American Christmas tradition is an evergreen in the parlor decorated with a multitude of colored lights and shining ornaments of gold and silver, a thing of wonder for all children. In the still of the night on Christmas Eve, however, the real significance of the tree can be felt. The Christmas tree was, and always will be, a symbol of Christ offering hope to all. ∎

It would be difficult, today, to think of Christmas without the presence of evergreens. If tradition did not ensure their decorative use, the visible beauty of the plants would. The use of plants at Christmas is one of the contributions made to Christianity by the pagans whose customs included greenery in many festivals and celebrations.

Ancient cultures had little scientific understanding of nature. They instead viewed many natural occurrences as magical phenomena. To their minds, nature and god were synonymous and omnipotent. Every towering pine, every crashing waterfall, every breaking tide, every thundering storm, every occurrence in nature, possessed mystical power. Early pagan use of greenery had little, if

anything, to do with decoration but with mysticism.

Bringing a piece of greenery into the home to add a touch of brightness and cheer is a custom thought to have begun in prehistoric times, and from the very beginning of recorded history, the evergreen has been a symbol of long life and immortality.

The Roman mid-December celebration of Saturnalia was founded in pagan customs, one of which was the gathering of greenery. Not wishing to draw attention to themselves, the early Christians also used greenery, and gradually the tradition was transformed from a pagan custom to a sacred one.

The early Christian church shunned the use of greenery as decoration because of its past link to pagandom, but eventually

Holly, Ivy, and Mistletoe

greenery gained acceptance among Christians because of a verse of Scripture from Isaiah: "The glory of Lebanon shall come unto thee, the fir tree, the pine tree, and the box together, to beautify the place of My sanctuary." So the early followers of Christ began to accept some of the pagan ideas and incorporate them into the methods of worship.

Mistletoe, the golden bough of classical legend, was early on considered sacred by the Norsemen and the Druids. Both cultures considered the plant a symbol of good luck and fertility, and they believed it protected their homes from witchcraft.

In Norse mythology, Balder, one of the best loved of all the gods, was killed by a mistletoe dart made under the direction of his jealous rival, Loki. Although Balder's mother, Frigga, was sad at the death of her son, she forgave the innocent mistletoe plant and made it the symbol of love. The ancient ceremony of kissing under the mistletoe in order to put an end to old grievances is based on Frigga's ability to forgive.

In early England, the annual harvesting of the mistletoe was an important and solemn practice. Druid priests directed the ritual and distributed branches of the parasite to their followers, who hung sprigs over the doorways to their homes. The Druids also believed that mistletoe contained curative qualities. Called *guildhel*, or "all heal," mistletoe was used in numerous old remedies to cure many ills.

Mistletoe was regarded in ancient Scandinavia as the plant

of peace under which enemies reconciled their differences and reached treaty agreements. Battles always ended if two opposing armies met under an oak tree filled with mistletoe. For centuries, underneath the branches of such trees, couples stood and embraced in hopes of achieving fertility and long life. The modern custom of kissing under the mistletoe came westward across the Atlantic from England. Where mistletoe hangs, a maiden standing under it cannot refuse a kiss.

Because of its importance in pagan tradition and its role in ancient mythology, mistletoe has received little acceptance in the Christian church as a Christmas decoration. Although very much a part of Christmas in the home, Christians generally avoid the use of mistletoe in their sanctuaries because it has no sacred purpose.

Holly, with its stiff, thorny leaves and bloodred berries, is thought by some to have been the plant from which Christ's crown of thorns was made. According to an old English legend, a robin plucked the sharp thorns from Christ's crown to relieve His suffering. As the legend goes, the Almighty then gave the robin its red breast. Holly berries are, indeed, a favorite food for robins, but the berries are poisonous for humans to eat.

Decking the halls with boughs of holly and ivy is a tradition that actually predates the Christmas tree. The use of greenery and garlands stems from the same ancient beliefs that made bringing a tree indoors such a popular event. Centuries ago, people thought of bringing in the branches as bringing home Christmas.

The Romans celebrated the approach of the new year as a time of rebirth, and greenery played a large role in their celebrations. Not only did they bring branches of evergreen inside, they fashioned branches into decorations for their outside light posts, and the boughs were twisted and wound into circles and hung on their doors.

The evergreens with berries were held in the highest regard, because they were seen as symbols of fertility. The popularity of the red-berried holly has evolved from both pagan and Christian uses and has been considered to have both bad powers and favorable ones. Its color has always made it a desirable decoration.

In areas where evergreens grow in abundance, they are often used in great quantities for decorations. Their boughs often line mantels and staircases. Holly, pine, and fir were abundant wild plants in colonial America and thus found their way into many homes.

The beautiful red and green poinsettia is the pot plant most closely associated with Christmas.

The ornamental shrub came to the attention of an amateur botanist, Dr. Joel Roberts Poinsett, during his tenure as American ambassador to Mexico from 1825 to 1829. So taken was Poinsett with the unusual plant that he brought samples back with him to his home in South Carolina, where he propagated cuttings for himself and for friends across the country. Eventually, the plant was named in his honor.

The actual flower of the poinsettia is a cluster of tiny red and gold blossoms. The small, true flowers lie in the center of a rosette of scarlet bracts that resemble petals. The bracts, like the plant's lush, forest green leaves, grow from a central stalk. Although the red poinsettias are traditional for the Christmas season, newer varieties have been commercially developed with bracts in various tints of pink or white.

Unlike mistletoe, the poinsettia

is not associated with either pagan customs or ancient mythology, and is, therefore, widely used during the Christmas season in both homes and churches.

Apart from the tree itself, the most common and widespread use of greenery for Christmas decoration is in wreaths. Like the twinkling lights of the tree in the living room window, the front door wreath extends an invitation to family and friends alike to come in from the cold and enjoy the warmth of good fellowship and good cheer. The traditional wreath of greenery tied with a bright red bow is a true American symbol of friendship and a message of welcome to all. ■

Christmas in this country without Santa Claus is now unthinkable. This most widely recognizable American figure is known to every man, woman, and child. By popular proclamation, he is the people's most exalted spreader of year-end holiday cheer. The round, jovial man in red, rosy cheeked and whiskered, sports soft white fur on his suit and cap. He may be seen on street corners and in malls from Thanksgiving Day to Christmas Eve. Then, very quickly, he returns to his North Pole toy factory from where he is able to cover the globe in one night. Hurrying from chimney to chimney in his sleigh pulled by flying reindeer, he delivers toys to the fireplaces of all good little girls and boys. This genuine, American-made patron of children emerged

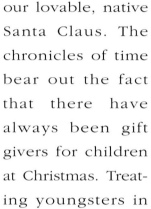

only about 125 years ago and grew out of many legends from the past.

Myth intertwined with history has given us the present version of our lovable, native Santa Claus. The chronicles of time bear out the fact that there have always been gift givers for children at Christmas. Treating youngsters in different lands for centuries were strange, mythical characters with odd names like Pelznichel, Knight Rupert, das Christkind, Kristkindlein, and Kriss Kringle. One in particular, Saint Nicholas, stands out as the major and most popular purveyor of seasonal gifts.

Saint Nicholas, however, was no legendary character. He actually lived during the fourth century. This noted bishop of Asia Minor gave freely of himself and was thought of as the patron saint of generosity. An outspoken church leader who was always willing to stand up against injustices, he was considered a man of conscience and compassion. During his lifetime, the old gentleman controlled an enormous amount of wealth, but willingly shared his fortune with those in need. His interest in all young people was genuine, but he had a particularly tender spot in his heart for maidens who could not marry for lack of an appropriate dowry.

As a secret gift giver, his good deeds were first found out by a poor nobleman who had three beautiful daughters. With no money for dowries, the daughters could not marry advantageously and their futures seemed hopeless. Anonymously, Nicholas attempted to save the trio of poverty-stricken young ladies from unhappy marriages by quiet-

ly tossing three bags of gold coins down the chimney of their home. And so it happened that one of the bags disruptively fell into a stocking hung by the fireplace to dry. The noisy saint was immediately discovered as he came off the roof.

News spread rapidly of the man's generosity. Soon, old Saint Nick received credit for any anonymous giving for which no explanation could be found.

Nicholas died in 343 A.D. Today, his remains may be visited in Antalya, Turkey, where a portrait of this great man also hangs. After his death, stories of the saint and his deeds spread northward through Europe. The accounts became legends filled with magic and miracles, and the tales grew and changed with every telling.

Quite by happenstance, an annual celebration, Saint Nicholas Day, originated with a Mother Superior and her group of convent schoolgirls. To illustrate points about faith and generosity, the Mother suggested that if the girls believed strongly enough, a stocking placed on their door knobs on December 6 might be filled with gifts to reward their faith. From that beginning, Saint Nicholas Day has since been observed in many countries.

Different nationalities have added to the original practice. The northern Europeans introduced a sleigh with fast-traveling reindeer. Saint Nick made his yearly visit to homes during the night, leaving presents in stockings and on white sheets which children spread before the fireplaces. The expectant youngsters themselves prepared and left out small cakes wrapped in thin, gold-leaf paper as a token repayment for the saint's goodness.

The Dutch brought Saint Nicholas to America when they settled New Amsterdam on that freezing Christmas Day in 1624. America gradually transformed Saint Nicholas into a plump, jolly old man with a sleigh filled with toys and pulled by eight tiny reindeer. In this country, his festive night ride changed from December 6 to Christmas Eve.

In spite of the Dutch settlers, New England Puritans continued to hold fast to their ban on a Christmas observance. Some Puritan families, however, may have held secret, quiet services in their homes. Some, perhaps, toasted the occasion, but there was little room in their stark, simple lifestyles for a Saint Nicholas of any sort.

As new colonial towns were settled side by side on the

JIM HARRISON

East coast, and as the Puritans gradually moved to other locations, the melting pot expanded. People all over the country began to learn of each other's holiday traditions and customs. It was very difficult to keep the excitement and joy of Santa Claus from reaching all children in America. Before long, regardless of religious background, all expected a visit from Santa Claus.

Nineteenth-century artists and writers created a wide variety of impressions of Santa and his activities. He was seen by most as a lovable, jolly fellow, very small in stature, with a big, generous heart. Washington Irving wrote of him in 1809 as a figure riding over rooftops and trees drawing forth magnificent presents from his breeches pockets and dropping them down chimneys. The most famous and enduring image of the jolly old man came from the pen of Dr. Clement Clark Moore. In 1822, the professor wrote a ballad which he read to a gathering of friends a few nights before Christmas. A member of the audience copied the words and sent the poem anonymously to the *Troy Sentinel*, where it was printed on December 23, 1823. "Twas the Night Before Christmas," as it later was entitled, gave Santa the added twinkle in his eyes and the dimples in his cheeks.

Santa retained his small, elfin image until 1931, when artist Haddon Sundblom was commissioned to create a Coca-Cola version of the old man. Sundblom's Santa became immediately popular. He appeared to be larger than life and has retained the likeness that we see today. It was Santa's union with Coca-Cola in the thirties that eventually sent his image around the globe in magazine ads and on billboards. Today, his warmth and good cheer are welcomed in all parts of the world. ∎

JIM HARRISON

Christmas time is toy time. For all the eager and expectant youngsters who are media blitzed with every newfangled plaything, it is a time of wants and wishes. High-powered advertising campaigns constantly plant the idea in naive, young minds that it is all right to expect almost anything from Santa's North Pole Work-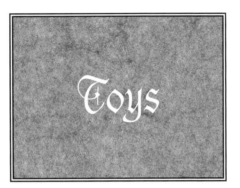

Toys

shop as he alone can reach into his bag and fetch out the desired toys. For toy makers, the Christmas season is the grand opportunity for sales, and they plan and prepare for months in advance of the year-end market. Each season, new ideas are developed, and expensive advertising campaigns are put in place.

Store-bought toys have not always been available in this country, and many a child was raised clinging to a homemade corn-husk doll or a hand-whittled oak slingshot. Today's technology and peer pressure have outpaced dad's ability to make toys, and he and his pocket-book have fallen prey to the power-ful toy sellers. The results so seriously damage the aver-age Christmas bud-get that most fami-lies' holiday pur-chases require the next twelve months to repay.

Some of the earliest and most amazing American homemade toys can be traced back several hundred years. The "gee-haw-whimmy-diddle" was made of two sticks that, when rubbed together, turned a propeller on the end of one of the sticks. By rubbing the sticks in the opposite direction, the direction of the propeller was changed. To this day, scientists are unable to explain the principle at work.

Most homemade toys of the seventeenth century were fashioned with a jackknife. Elderberry twigs were turned into pop guns, whistles were carved from chestnut wood, and windmills and waterwheels were favorite items for the front-porch toy maker.

A good pocketknife was the key to craft. Barlow's knives from England were the best and were prized by anyone who owned one. A young whittler made clubs, slingshots, animals, and bows and arrows for himself and his younger brothers and sisters.

Many items found around the farm became materials for toys. Corn husks were made into dolls, and the cobs could be stacked as play logs to make houses and forts. Early marbles were shaped from barnyard clay and hardened by the sun.

Store-bought toys were unknown in America before 1850. As the country approached the Civil War era, however, toy stores began to spring up everywhere. Big city stores turned into toylands at Christmas, and merchants piled their shelves high with imported toys of every description.

Very popular during the post–Civil War period was a plaything known as the Sunday toy, Noah's Ark. From colonial times and into the early twentieth century, it was the custom for toys to be put away on the Sabbath. Noah's Ark, however, was the exception. Because of the toy's religious background, it was acceptable for young ones to bring it out on the day of rest.

Many a time, the rather large ark was found not to be seaworthy by the youngsters who dared test it in water. The ark itself served as a container for the many animals that were stuffed in under the roof. When the roof was lifted off, Noah and his family were found inside along with more than three hundred beasts, birds, and insects. The contents of the ark were painted in such accurate detail that the differences between male and female were made distinct. Sizes were not all too accurate, however, as a fly might be one-third the size of an elephant. Although all of God's creatures were out of proportion each to the other, all had their own special appeal as they were taken one by one, or two by two, from the interior of the ark.

In the days following the Civil War, iron and tin came into common use for toy making. There were miniature railroad engines, cheap tin watches, and mechanical cast-iron banks. Model automobiles, kiddie cars, bicycles, tricycles, and roller skates provided fun on wheels. India rubber was used to make balls and doll heads. Balloons were designed in various animal shapes. Roosters and parrots were designed so that they made different sounds as air escaped from the balloons.

Children loved toys that incorporated sound and motion. In the early twentieth century, an avalanche of such toys was affordable to almost every budget. Jack-in-the-boxes, pop guns, and cannons that fired dried corn were available. Doll babies that cried, dogs that barked, music boxes, and wind-up toys were being produced in quantity.

In 1875, the Ehrich toy store in New York City displayed a very popular, life-size doll that cried and had its own stroller. The Ehrich brothers always had the

finest and most complete line of playthings which, for the most part, were imported from Europe. The Christmas season always brought out the best in the designers, and the Ehrichs prided themselves in having the newest of everything.

The French and the Germans excelled at making mechanical toys, and each Christmas would bring out a new line of fascinating examples. As early as 1887, there were electric trains, steamboats, and cast-iron replicas of any and all forms of machinery and transportation. The turn of the twentieth century brought with it toy automobiles that ran and planes that actually flew. Some of these elaborate models cost as much as one hundred dollars.

The 1902 Christmas line introduced an airship that hung from the ceiling and circled around and around, propelled by a wound-up rubber band. A submarine, oper-

ated by a steel spring wound with a key, ran a distance on the surface of the water and then submerged when weight shifted its position. As the weight shifted back, it would return to the surface. Each year, the manufacturers seemed to exceed themselves in trying to top the previous year's introductions. In 1903, a battery-operated telephone set permitted children to talk from one room to the next. It seemed toys were becoming too clever, and, in fact, toy makers did unveil mechanical innovations that became the basis for everyday adult products. From the beginning of the twentieth century, the toy business boomed to where it is today.

Dolls were being improved every year, too. Heads, arms, and legs were fashioned from bisque colored with flesh tones. Facial features were molded more clearly and included lifelike hair. All kinds of accessories accompanied the more expensive dolls and, for most families, proved to be quite an investment.

Parents would refurbish, redress, and add new accessories to last year's doll to go under this year's Christmas tree. Manipulating the doll away from home for the refurbishing and having it appear again Christmas morning was quite a task for any parent. Store owners assisted with the deception and established pickup stations under the pretense that the old doll was being sent to Santa's Workshop for the redoing.

R. H. Macy's department store became a national pace-setting toy merchandiser. The store had a toyland so complete that parents could leave children in the care of employees while they shopped in other departments.

Toys reflected the events of the times and the personalities of the day, such as the toy that grew out of this famous incident. In November 1902, President Teddy Roosevelt went to Mississippi to settle a boundary line dispute between that state and Louisiana. The President was a sportsman, so even though he was on official business he took time out to do some bear hunting. It was reported that he spotted a bear, took aim, but refused to shoot when he realized the bear was a small cub.

Clifton Berryman, a political cartoonist for the *Washington Post*, seized the opportunity and did a panel which portrayed the President's warm, human side. The cartoon, entitled "Drawing the Line in Mississippi," appeared in many papers across the country and became an item of conversation.

The hunting incident sparked the imagination of a Brooklyn toy maker, Morris Michtom. Michtom and his wife cut a pattern of a bear, sewed it up, and used buttons for eyes. Morris then placed the bear in his shop window along with a copy of the cartoon and a sign reading "Teddy's Bear." The toy maker quickly sold the bear and immediately realized the potential of his product. He wrote to the president and asked permission to use his name. Roosevelt jokingly commented that his name had no financial value, so he willingly gave permission without charge. Later, the Michtom family toy business developed into the Ideal Toy Company; today, it is one of the country's leading producers of teddy bears and dolls.

In the past half century, alone, two hundred million teddy bears have been sold, and "Teddy" is now an American legend loved by tots, teens, and adults alike. Teddy Roosevelt's namesake has become a true American collectible, and it is the universal toy of the world.

Contemporary toys reflect the world's advanced state of technology. By using the wonders of science, today's toys offer not only entertainment but learning opportunities as well. Wind-up toys of the past have been replaced by complicated electronic games and computer devices. Under the modern American Christmas tree toys and games can be found that involve the entire family and present rather stiff challenges, even for the adults. ∎

A custom among some children is to welcome and attempt to guide Santa Claus with an array of fireworks on the night of his world travels. Many families gather on Christmas Eve to watch as a variety of small fireworks are fired off by their youngsters.

Firecrackers

The "shooting" of the safer, home varieties in no way equals the huge, professional, public displays on New Year's Eve and July 4. Christmas Eve takes its place third in line behind the commercial extravaganzas that usher in another year or celebrate America's independence.

There is no evidence to document who was actually the first person to make fireworks. The art of pyrotechnics probably happened by accident, and most historians attribute the earliest experiments to the Chinese. A book believed to have been written in 49 A.D. describes the use of gunpowder to make a small firecracker-like "fire pill." A bamboo tube was packed with finely ground charcoal and sulfur with a fuse attached. This early firecracker produced only a flash of fire and smoke with no explosive bang.

The discovery of gunpowder also remains a mystery, but some legends concerning its origin have been repeated for centuries. One story goes that a cook noticed that when potassium nitrate, a form of cooking salt, spilled under the cooking pot the fire grew brighter and caused a small explosion. Perhaps tribesmen, as they sat around open fires, detected that when salt dropped into the fire the flame burned brighter.

It was also discovered that if the rock that lined a fire pit contained sulfur, the combination of charcoal and potassium nitrate with the sulfur caused a small explosion.

By the fourteenth century, a consistent gunpowder was being made by mixing ground charcoal with sulfur and potassium nitrate. An abundance of charcoal was easily produced by controlling the amount of oxygen available for burning wood.

For centuries, the world went wild producing gunpowder and advancing its use as a military weapon. As firearms of all descriptions were developed, the military arsenals of most civilized countries grew. Those military men who became experts in the handling and firing of gunpowder also contributed to the development of less powerful fireworks.

When an army won a battle, the gunpowder experts were asked to provide a fireworks display as part of the victory celebration. The explosive handlers could adjust the fuses in a variety of ways to have the rockets burst in the air rather than explode on the ground. Cannon salutes, double-action rockets, and pinwheels became popular devices shot into the air for the enjoyment of celebrating armies.

The job of putting on victory displays became so important that fireworks specialists, called pyrotechnicians, were trained for the task, and official military manuals were written detailing instructions about fireworks procedures. Gradually, aerial displays became very elaborate, and kings would order firework shows for special festive events. So knowledgeable were the display experts that detailed images of monarchs, heroes, flags, and bells could be devised as pictures painted in pyrotechnic eloquence.

Through the centuries, fireworks

displays, their uses, and their sponsors have changed. Kings and rulers are no longer the patrons. Today, agricultural fairs have huge fireworks displays, military bases have similar holiday attractions, and theme parks entertain their visitors daily with nighttime shows. As commercial promotions, department stores, banks, civic clubs, athletic events, shopping malls, and newspapers sponsor fireworks "shootings."

Through two centuries of use, fireworks have become more powerful and more dangerous, yet they remain one of the most enduring customs. They are very much enjoyed by young and old around the world.

One of today's most popular and safest varieties is the sparkler, a piece of steel wire coated with combustible chemicals. When ignited with a match the chemicals burn brightly at a temperature of about 1650°F and should be handled with care. The flaming sparkler gives off a shower of white, red, green, and gold sparks as it is held by hand and waved in a circular motion.

Snakes and worms are among the favorite home fireworks. A small packet of chemicals, tightly wrapped in cardboard or foil, is ignited. As the mixture slowly burns, a long trail of gray ash is produced. Because this ash snake becomes larger than its container, the ashes are slowly pushed out in the manner of a snake or worm crawling out of a hole.

Roman candles are long tubes filled with both burning and exploding powder. They may be hand held, stuck in the ground, or placed in a container. When lit, each layer of powder explodes and shoots a series of flaming stars some twelve to fifteen feet in the air. The stars, in reality, are tightly packed balls of chemicals that burn as they fly. Between the launching of each star, a fountain of sparks is emitted from the tube.

Rockets look similar to Roman candles, but they perform quite differently. The tube of the rocket is attached to a long stick which is usually stuck in the ground or in a bottle. The tube is designed with a cone on top to stabilize its flight. Burning gunpowder inside the tube produces a gas that escapes through a small hole at the rear of the rocket and pushes the rocket through the air. A second, slower-burning fuse causes the rocket to explode at a certain height, scattering burning stars and sparks that fly in all directions.

Firecrackers are made the same way as rockets except they provide no way for the burning gas to escape. A slender, paper tube one to two inches long is packed with powder. A fuse extends from the tube for several inches to allow for safe lighting. Just as in the rocket, the burning gas pushes out in all directions, but the end of the tube is sealed. The pressure of the gas is great enough to blow the tube apart which produces a loud noise. Usually, a number of firecrackers are strung together and explode in sequence, one after the other.

The visually colorful fountain is similar to a rocket except the fountain is shaped with a pointed top and is attached to a wooden base. Sparks and burning chemicals are forced out of a small opening at the top, erupting somewhat like a volcano. Rather than propelling the container upward, a reverse action is produced, and the escaping gases are propelled upward from the fountain which remains stationary on the ground. The result is a flaming, colorful fountain of flying sparks and burning gunpowder.

Because of the dangers of injury and fire, government regulations control the sale and "shooting" of fireworks today. Large, outdoor firework exhibitions, which are held for large audiences, are approved only if they are rigged and set off by experts who are trained to handle the dangerous explosives. Contemporary, outdoor displays include wheels and pinwheels propelled by rockets attached to spinning devices on frames. Instead of flying through the air, the rockets push the wheels, causing a circular display. Other explosives are shot into the air from a cannonlike fixture and explode loudly at their highest point like a rocket, sending stars and other explosives with delayed fuses in every direction.

Whatever the fascination with watching a waving sparkler, a bursting firecracker, or a dark sky suddenly ablaze and alive with dazzling light, color, and sound, fireworks are a lasting part of the Christmas event. No doubt their early use was pagan in origin, as noise and spectacle lent themselves to the more boisterous celebrations of old. Today's stamp of approval and appreciation for the science of pyrotechnics, however, can best be acknowledged by noting the number of Christian churches that include a family night of fireworks as a part of the Christmas season. ■

Annually, two billion Christmas cards help those Americans who cannot put their sentiments in appropriate words express "Merry Christmas and Happy New Year." In this country, the December custom is slightly more than one hundred years old. Cards are the most popular holiday messengers around the world, and they  distribute best wishes and good cheer from friend to friend and family to family.

The practice of written seasonal greetings began with the ancient Egyptians and Romans, who exchanged respects and best wishes as each new year began. During those imperial days of Roman history, citizens reminded friends of their love for them, and government officials assured the emperor of their loyalty and obe-dience by sending gifts on the day of the New Year.

Originally, the presents were rather elaborate, but gradually they were reduced to small clay tablets upon which were written sea-sonal messages. Often, the tablets were decorated with borders of fruit and garlands surrounding such messages as "Hap-piness in the New Year." The Christian church of that era opposed the worldly, heathen habit of gift giving but was more permissive with the custom of the New Year's greeting card. Later, in medieval Europe, artists and printmakers worked togeth-er to fashion Bible passages with religious scenes on woodblock prints as a means of issuing the annual best wishes. Expressions of love and good luck often accompanied the illustrations and greetings.

Children's Christmas pieces were a forerunner of the first English greeting cards. Tremendous emphasis was placed on the teaching of penmanship in nineteenth-century schools. Prior to the year-end holidays, schoolmasters had children prepare seasonal greetings to take home as gifts for their parents. The children wrote in the elaborate script of the time and illuminated their compositions with drawings of birds and animals.

The Christmas card itself was developed out of necessity in 1843 when Sir Henry Cole, an English gentleman of many interests and talents, realized that he owed too many seasonal notes for him to write by hand. In Cole's nineteenth-century England it was the custom for friends to deliver personal notes of good cheer at Christmas and the New Year. Often, these took the form of visiting cards with handwritten messages on them.

Cole's innovative solution, originally intended just for his own use, became the first Christmas card. He engaged the services of an artist, John Calcott Horsley, R.A., to create a layout carrying a dual seasonal message. The now familiar "A Merry Christmas and a Happy New Year to you" was lithographed in a limited edition of one thousand colored cards. Not only did the cards resolve Mr. Cole's social predicament, he decided to place the unused cards for sale in his art shop.

The Cole-Horsley card was well designed in the style of the book illustrations of the time. Trellis work and garlands of ivy created a frame around a triptych design illustrating a happy family gathering of good eating, good drinking, and good cheer. The caption seemed to invite the recipient to join in both the Christmas spirit

JIM HARRISON

and the New Year beginning. This was the first known time that the two wishes were combined together. The 3-by-5-inch card was printed only on one side and was designed so that the addressee's name could be written at the top and the signature of the sender placed at the bottom. It is interesting to note that Christmas was gaining popularity during the middle years of the nineteenth century and the cards sold very well, but Cole's innocent conception stirred up wrath in the religious community. The objection of the Puritans was to be expected; they were distressed by the Horsley illustration, which they thought depicted too much festivity.

In his own way, Cole had an ongoing mission in life to revive arts and crafts from their suffering position created by the onslaught of the Industrial Revolution. Through his art shop named Felix Summerly he worked toward that goal, and he actively supported living artists. Commissioning Horsley to illustrate his card was a part of that effort. Cole was a religious man, however, with no interest in disrupting the church. Never again did he produce a card, and there was no immediate successor.

Several years passed before some Englishmen independently produced various cards, and a few companies that printed playing cards, note cards, and valentines added the yuletide version as a sideline. It was not until 1867 that Marcus Ward and Company began publishing seasonal greeting cards as their main line, putting all of their abilities into Christmas designs. A variety of small cards, the size of visiting cards, was developed and became very popular. By the 1870s, English cards were being imported and sold extensively in the United States.

It was a German-born immigrant, Louis Prang, who first saw the possibilities for producing Christmas cards in America. The young man had settled in Boston to learn the trade of printing and wood engraving. Earlier, Prang had been frustrated as an aspiring artist, but he still maintained a keen interest in fine art. In his Boston shop, he developed a greatly improved method of color printing.

Prang displayed his new chromolithography at the Vienna world exhibition of 1873. While there, he handed out business cards on which he had printed realistic colorful flowers. The cards became instantly popular because of their lifelike design and color. The young artisan was encouraged by some European friends to print similar cards with Christmas greetings on them.

In 1874, Prang produced for export to England a selection of cards depicting famous paintings combined with seasonal greetings. They were so well received that he made plans for marketing Christmas cards in America the next year. The timing was right and circumstances were such for his cards to succeed. Prior to 1863 there had been no free mail delivery. The recipient of a letter or card had to pay for delivery or go to the post office and pick it up. In 1863, the federal government, at the urging of President Abraham Lincoln, established free mail delivery in the big cities. Door-to-door mail service naturally spurred the use and sale of Christmas cards.

Prang's enthusiasm for art was reflected in his Christmas card business. In 1881, in an effort to attract the best artists, he started an annual design contest. He offered cash prices of as much as one thousand dollars for first place, and he arranged with the

American Art Gallery in New York for a formal showing of the entered designs. This popular event brought fine art and Christmas card design together and attracted the attention and favor of the public. More serious artists began to create new and refreshing Christmas card designs, and Prang encouraged their creativity by featuring the art in an enlarged seven-by-ten-inch format. The image was printed on the outside with the message and a short biography of the artist on the inside.

The card messages included poetry, rhymes, and short prose. First and foremost, Prang strove for quality, and he exerted every measure to make his cards the best they could be. Prang cards exhibited excellent color, and as many as twenty separate plates were used in the printing. The cards sold for the high price of one dollar each, but millions of them were marketed. Prang never compromised either his price or his quality.

In the early 1900s, names like the Gibson Art Company and the Davis Company entered the card market. Also, very plentiful at that time was a multitude of less expensive postcards imported from England and Germany. Those were offered in a variety of versions. Novelty cards with lace edges, embossed centers, tassels, and perfume scent were faddish, but popular. There were pop-up cards depicting children singing and horse-drawn sleighs dashing through the snow. Cards came in all shapes and innovations, including ones with buttons to press so that the sounds of Christmas could be heard. The illustrations and messages of this period did not usually portray religious motifs, nor did they refer to the holiday as a Christian observance. Card sending was strictly a secular activity. The variety of illustrations included flowers, plants, sea shells, butterflies, and birds. The popularity of nature subjects most probably had to do with the coming of spring and the promise of renewal.

In the late 1800s, enterprising American newspaper boys presented their customers with a Christmas address. Poems wishing happiness and incorporating subtle hints for tips were written by the enterprising lads. And the idea of addresses without mention of tips became popular with mailmen, lamplighters, waiters, and others who served the public.

By the early part of the nineteenth century, George Eastman had developed the simple push-button camera and the photographic developing process to the point where everyone could become a photographer. As early as 1902, his company, Eastman Kodak, offered customers the opportunity to have their photographs printed on greeting cards. Family group portraits became a fashionable way to deliver the seasonal message.

In 1910, a young man named Joyce C. Hall was importing cards from Europe and selling them to merchants in the Kansas City area. He and his two brothers opened a specialty card and stationary store, but a fire burned the business and all of the inventory. Undaunted, the determined Hall brothers came back even stronger. They purchased an engraving company, produced their own cards, and Hallmark Greeting Cards was born. Today, with Hallmark stores in every major mall in America, the company offers some 2,500 Christmas card designs each year and a wide variety of other greeting cards and gift items.

Gradually, twentieth-century cards began to include designs and subjects that reflected the times. While the older themes remained popular, a drastically new innovation was the very popular humorous card. Any collection of American Christmas cards reveals the trends, the social changes, and the current events of the times. The first World War interrupted the importation of European cards and marked the beginning of tremendous growth in the American card business. The war itself created a great demand for cards. Families were separated and seasonal cards carried messages of love, hugs, and kisses from loved ones at home to soldiers away at war.

The good times of the roaring twenties were reflected by flappers doin' the Charleston and Santa Claus delivering toys in sporty roadsters. Cards of the thirties made light of the depression, and featured messages and scenes of hope for better times. The 1940s cards again reflected the disruption of war with loved ones separated from one another. Patriotism was most evident in many designs.

With the 1950s came the cold war, the popularity of television, and the American Space Program. Santa Claus was pictured on Christmas cards as traveling around the globe on a rocket or stretched out in front of his North Pole television set.

The 1960s and the 1970s saw the coming of age of the baby boomers. Their cards reflected a sense of idealism, a search for peace, and the spreading of love. Peace symbols, doves, and flower children from around the world adorned this generation's Christmas messengers. The cards of the 1980s returned humor and nostalgia to the available selections. Religious cards with a strong contemporary look were popular.

Each new decade brings with it change, and the American Christmas card, too, has ridden the waves of style and fashion. It has escaped neither the fads nor the gimmicks, but some things are here to stay. Santa in a sleigh, bright Christmas trees, stockings by the fireplace, and silent snow scenes joined by "Merry Christmas and Happy New Year" say it all. ∎

Christmas is a time of lights. Churches and homes alike are ablaze with candles at Christmas, and the flickering flames are a reminder that Jesus Christ was born to be the Light of the World.

The custom of displaying lighted candles in windows is a carry-over from earlier cultures that believed the Christ child could be guided through the darkness to those houses which lit His way. It was also thought that Christ might disguise Himself and approach a home in order to determine the sincerity of its occupants. The candles served as a sign of welcome to all, and no stranger who desired to enter was ever turned away for any reason.

Churches, too, had their superstitions. It was once considered proper only for a female named Mary to extinguish Christmas candles that had been lit in the church. At one time, Christians believed that the candles used in the sanctuaries must be made of pure beeswax. Beeswax is made by virgin bees, and churchgoers believed those bees were sent directly from heaven to perform this deed.

Candles were used sparingly as a source of light throughout the home all year long. But at Christmas time, for decorative purposes, additional ones were placed on mantels, tables, walls, and even the tree. They were once the only source of light on the tree, but since have been replaced by small electric light bulbs.

The risk of fire with candlelit trees was great. Beeswax and bayberry wax candles were less flammable than candles made from tallow and therefore were considered to be safer. Home candle makers further reduced the fire risk by tapering their candles to make them more stable, and the hot, dripping tallow was minimized by designing them with a spiral shape. A three-pronged candle holder, to represent the three Wise Men, was sometime made and placed at the top of the tree.

The yule candle came into its own during the latter half of the nineteenth century and was widely used in most households. Its popularity was insured by a practice started by local food merchants. As a Christmas gift to regular customers, grocers would deliver a candle with the family's food order.

The custom was to burn the yule candle on Christmas Day. Should it be allowed to go out, the household could prepare for a run of bad luck during the coming year. The candle, therefore, was purposely quite large, and once it was

lit, no one was allowed to touch it. The head of the household or the oldest family member present was given the honor of putting it out at the appropriate time. In earlier years, the candles were lit from the blaze of the yule log. According to legend, as those special Christmas candles burned they radiated special blessings. Many items such as food and clothing were spread out in front of the candles so their rays would strike and sanctify the items.

Long before candles came into use, the fireplace was the only source of light in the home at night. Candles appeared much later in history. Even though candles were more convenient and more efficient, they did not replace the cozy glow of a fire in an old-time fireplace.

A centrally located fireplace not only provided heat and light in the home, it was also the family's main gathering place. The hearth was the heart of the home, and the roughness of cold winters outside reinforced the comfort of gathering around a roaring fire. Other forms of heat today may better warm the home, but only the fireplace warms both the hands and heart. Happier was the home with an open hearth where families gathered for conversation and fellowship, to do indoor chores, and to play games.

Part of the charm of Christmas and its celebration lies in its winter setting. In many parts of the country, frost is on the window and snow is on the ground—no wonder, then, that a favorite custom of past times was the yule log. The burning of the log was welcomed in the home not only for its cozy warmth but also for the light and gaiety that it added to the room.

Historians point to Scandinavia as the origin of the ancient custom of burning the yule log. At the feast of the winter solstice, the Scandinavians built huge bonfires to "burn the Juul" in honor of their god, Thor.

They believed the sun was attached to a big wheel which stopped for twelve days during the winter solstice. The people assumed it was up to them to keep bonfires going during the twelve-day interval. In many European countries today, true Christmas begins at midnight on December 24 and lasts until Twelfth Night, the eve of Epiphany.

In England, the bringing in and burning of the yule log on Christmas Eve was a rather elaborate occasion. According to custom, the log was carefully selected months before Christmas. On the night before Christmas, the huge logs were drawn into the castles with great fanfare and music. The larger, more wealthy estates engaged minstrels to entertain. If entertainers were unavailable or unaffordable, members of the family would take their turn in saluting the log with singing and toasting. When the fire eventually died, the remnant of the log was kept until the next year to be used to kindle the new log. The unburned portion of the old log was stored near the fireplace to serve as a protector against lightning.

The ashes also were saved because they had an important purpose; according to ancient belief, they possessed curing and healing powers for both men and cattle. Some cultures believed that if the ashes were scattered over the fields the ground would be richer and yield better crops.

The yule-log custom in America was quite prevalent on the huge agricultural plantations. The slaves

JIM HARRISON

were granted freedom from work for just as long as the log burned. There was considerable excitement and expertise as the older hands searched for the right log. A hardwood usually was the best candidate. If the tree was felled in time, the slaves would soak the log slightly with water to ensure a slower and longer burning time. Bringing in the yule log was a festive day accompanied by the musical spirituals of the time. The actual lighting of the log was considered the highest honor of the year bestowed to a servant; it was usually reserved for the oldest field hand "on the place." Other parts of America enjoyed the yule log, but none with the fanfare of the Southern plantation.

Today's modern homes, with their smaller fireplaces and artificial gas logs, cannot accommodate a log of great size, so the custom is hardly practical anywhere now. Gone with the custom is a sizable part of the Christmas romance. ■

Festivals of all ages have included music and singing to celebrate particular joyous events. The early Greeks and Romans from time to time honored their gods and leaders with testimonial hymns and community singing.

Most historians agree that Christmas celebrations began around 129 A.D., and evidence suggests that the earliest observances included carols. Many of the songs sung today are more recent in origin, but some have been handed down for centuries from one generation to the next. The exact sources of most of the older melodies are unknown. The earliest carols were in Latin and were included in the Nativity plays when Latin was a spoken language. Others were sung by traveling minstrels who went from village to village earning money as entertainers. The villagers, long afterwards, continued to sing the lyrics and passed them down to their children by repeating them from memory year after year. These age-old songs were sung, enjoyed, and even modified for centuries before anyone thought to write them down.

St. Francis of Assisi promoted the idea of writing music and lyrics for the Christmas season. So great was his enthusiasm and involvement that he is credited as being the Father of the Christmas Carol.

The various Christian countries all have their own unique backgrounds of Christmas music. In medieval England, traveling troubadours went from castle to castle entertaining the lords of the manors, for a fee, with their versions of the season's music. Religious songs made up part of the programs, but more often the selections were light and kept the spirit of merrymaking.

In England and in the American colonies, the strict Pilgrim fathers forbade any form of revelry or singing. In other parts of the colonies, however, the settlers enjoyed making the music they had brought with them from the Old World.

Today, at Christmastime, millions of voices are raised the world over to herald the glad tidings of comfort and joy. Music and singing offer the most natural human expression for the peace, hope, and wonder of the Christmas spirit. The season would be rather somber without the happy sound of music.

The greatest composers of every age have contributed to the vast collection of Christmas music. Handel's great oratorio, the *Messiah*, continues after hundreds of years to be presented annually in communities around the world, and Tchaikovsky's ballet, *The Nutcracker*, is enjoyed by both children and adults of all nationalities. The genius of such composers is unquestioned, and they will always have their exalted place in the timeless catalog of Christmas music. However, these magnificent compositions were written to be sung and performed by professionals, and untrained musicians and singers cannot adequately execute the complexities of these works.

More practical music for most people to sing and enjoy during the season are Christmas carols. These simple, popular songs have broad universal appeal with melodies and lyrics that most anyone can follow and enjoy, and most require only a limited vocal range on the musical scale.

Christmas is a time for family, friends, and neighbors to gather around crackling fireplaces and twinkling trees to spontaneously join in song. It is here at the hearth, as well as at the great, public performances of the oratorios and ballets, that the spirit of the season may be found. Community Christmas trees also give folks a chance to gather together and serenade the season.

Department stores encourage shopper sing-alongs, and school glee clubs and church choirs perform at center court in most malls. Small groups of cheerful singers visit shut-ins, hospitals, and prisons. Strolling carolers travel from house to house with their Christmas melodies drifting throughout the neighborhoods and the cool night air. And more often than not, appreciative listeners reward the singers with hot chocolate, cider, or coffee.

America has accumulated a vast collection of native Christmas music, but, as with all customs, some of the best-loved carols come directly from other countries. The English carol "Good King Wenceslas" sets to music the story of a kind, caring master who walked ahead of his servants in the snow to warm a path with his footprints so that his subordinates could better endure the bitter weather. The British also sent us "God Rest Ye Merry Gentlemen" who still bring "tidings of comfort and joy."

The first Christmas hymns and carols recorded, in music, the details of the birth of Christ. The Nativity scene, the manger, the three kings, the animals in the stable, and the bright star were all a part of the musical message. Songs also memorialize the angels who "were heard on

high." The earliest known carol, "O Come, O Come, Emmanuel," is still very popular today, even though it dates from the Middle Ages. Perhaps the years of its singing have incorporated some changes and improvements.

A few of the world's most famous composers have created some of Christmas's most beloved carols. George Frederic Handel, the composer of the *Messiah*, wrote the music for "Joy to the World," and Felix Mendelssohn, known for his wedding march, is credited with "Hark the Herald Angels Sing."

For years, Martin Luther was credited with writing one of the best-loved Christmas songs, "Away in a Manger." Supposedly, he composed the hymn for his children, but English history now has some evidence to dispute his authorship. An American, James Pierport, currently is believed to be the author. This Southern songwriter wrote patriotic tunes to rally the Confederates during the Civil War, and he also painted a pretty picture of a one-horse open sleigh with his lyrics and music for "Jingle Bells."

Some Christmas carols have poignant stories behind them. Episcopal rector Philip Brooks of Philadelphia visited the Church of the Nativity in Bethlehem on Christmas Eve, 1865. The minister was so moved by his experience that when he returned to Pennsylvania he wrote "O Little Town of Bethlehem." In the small Alpine village of Oberndorf, choir director Frank Grubee discovered on the eve before the Christmas cantata that the church organ was broken. During the night he composed "Silent Night," and the next day, with his guitar accompanying him, he sang the everlasting carol to his church congregation.

Not all Christmas music, however, is religious. Christmas gaiety is set to contemporary music, and many of the older carols were written as tunes created for dancing on Christmas Day. Dancing, as part of the celebration, has vanished, but the music of that time has survived. "Deck the Halls" and "We Wish You a Merry Christmas" are sung today as lively tunes expressing the happiness and cheerfulness of the season.

More recent carols are about family celebrations, secular activities, and beloved traditions. The building of snow men, sleigh rides, and Santa Claus are featured in many modern songs, such as "Here Comes Santa Claus," "Santa Claus Is Coming to Town," and "Rudolph the Red-Nosed Reindeer."

From New York's Broadway theaters and from the movies came "Winter Wonderland" and "Let It Snow! Let It Snow! Let It Snow!" In 1942, the film *Holiday Inn* included a song composed by Irving Berlin entitled "White Christmas." Made famous by crooner Bing Crosby, it has become the best-selling Christmas song of all time.

During World War II, Christmas music adapted to the circumstances. For several Christmas seasons, "I'll Be Home for Christmas" expressed the wishes and hopes of the soldiers who were away from home. Occasional humorous songs such as "All I Want for Christmas Is My Two Front Teeth" remained popular for years.

No one can predict which of the contemporary songs will endure. Those that have lasted for centuries have proven the test of time and will be a part of the celebration forever. New music freshens the songbook of carols each season. Some will last; some will not. From the very beginning, Christmas has brought with it seasonal melodies and singing, and for as long as the event is celebrated there will be music in the air. ∎

Out of necessity, early Americans combined Old World traditions with the native foods of the New World. As with most American Christmas customs, our forebears' holiday eating habits originated in Europe and traveled across the Atlantic with them. The variety of tastes and dishes were as broad as the number of countries from which the settlers came.

The more affluent English immigrants held fast to their mother-country traditions. On Christmas Day, they sat down to a feast of Southdown mutton and capons imported from Liverpool, sirloin of beef, or roasted goose. Brussels sprouts, beets, boiled onions, and roasted chestnuts in plentiful supply complimented the main dish. Traditional dessert offerings included mince pie and the plump, round plum pudding.

English housewives treasured and guarded their secret recipes for the very popular plum pudding, and each one believed hers to be the best in the world. Made from beef or lamb fat, flour, and raisins spiced with brandy, the pudding took days to prepare. Superstition holds to this day that bad luck will befall any family member who does not stir the mixture. When thoroughly prepared to the right consistency, the pudding traditionally was hand shaped into a ball, wrapped in a square yard of strong, unbleached muslin, and hung up for several weeks to ferment. On Christmas Eve, the alcoholic delight was taken down and steamed all night for the next day's feast. A last-minute dousing

with either rum or brandy provided the fuel for the pudding's flaming entrance from the kitchen.

The Germans, more than any of the other newcomers, zealously wanted their Christmas celebrations to be *gerade wie in Deutschland*, "the same as in Germany." Imported boar and innumerable kinds of sausages were the choices of most families, but the smokehouses of the fatherland also provided very popular delicacies like goose breast and peacock. Like the English, they, too, had a plum duff, plus apple and pear butters and numerous jams and honeys often eaten with meat.

The Germans had a passion for sweets and pastries. Cooks would outdo themselves making elaborate centerpieces of gingerbread houses and castles, complete with icing snow on the roofs. Included in the setting were gingerbread people, animals, fences, and mail-boxes. Baskets, overflowing with a variety of sugar and almond-paste cookies, were provided for the children. Food coloring and icing added realistic touches to the marzipan shapes of fruits and toys. To this day, many a sweet tooth is satisfied by the recipes from those early German kitchens.

Settlers in the American wilderness lived almost totally from the land. They had no peacocks or capons to feast upon, but an abundance of wild turkeys filled in adequately. On backcountry Christmas tables, the turkey was joined by roasted wild duck, deer, and fish. Eventually, the settlers had hams, beef, and whole, roasted suckling pigs to set upon the holiday table.

Oddly enough, the turkey eventually gained the widest acceptance as the main American Christmas dish. The wild bird is native to America, and huge flocks roamed the woods of the

New World. They stood some two to three feet tall and weighed up to thirty pounds. A large turkey provided a plentiful supply of both white and dark meat.

In the wild, turkeys are very keen and difficult to hunt. They make for an interesting challenge to backwoods hunters. The placement of the bird's eyes allow it to see an area of three hundred degrees. A strong sense of smell and sound coupled with its speed afoot add to its natural defenses.

Baked to a golden brown and with the addition of cornbread dressing and giblet gravy, the turkey became the traditional American holiday food. Cranberry sauce, candied yams, corn, and pumpkin pie are decidedly American accompaniments. Rich fruitcakes and fluffy coconut cakes paired with sweet fruit ambrosia are basic Christmas desserts in most parts of this country.

So important a food was the humble turkey to America's survival that Benjamin Franklin promoted it as our national symbol. The noble eagle eventually was selected, and now it flies the skies unharmed and protected by Federal laws. Much to the turkey's disadvantage, however—the latter became our national Christmas dinner.

Not all people, of course, relied upon the turkey, and today, in some sections of the United States, one still can find Christmas foods that are prepared from old recipes directly linked to the early settlers of the particular area. Too, different regions still reflect the influences of other cultures and cuisines brought to this country by the immigrants.

In the Midwest and Northwest, Scandinavian descendants sit down to a yuletide dish of salted fish or smoked salmon served with warm apple cider. A Mexican flair prevails in the West, and the smell of sweet tamales and posole fill many a Christmas dining room.

Today's store-bought foods and high-tech advancements provide the microwave capabilities of preparing a meal in minutes. The Christmas feast of the mid-eighteenth century was a major part of the festivities, and it actually required months of advance planning, preparation, and cooking. Usually, it was the single largest family gathering of the year.

American Christmas practices in years past found the next year's celebration beginning in some kitchens as soon as the old year ended. Mincemeat, fruit cakes, wine, and puddings were all made months ahead so that they could age and mellow.

Fruitcake tins or, more often, large lard cans were used to store and age the cakes. On a regular schedule, the tins were opened and each cheesecloth-wrapped cake would get a good dousing of strong Christmas cheer in the form of rum or brandy. Originally, mincemeat mixtures also included an abundant measure of spirits, which also would get additional kickers periodically.

Today's popular holiday punch bowl, with its many rounds of seasonal toasts, came to America from the apple orchards of eighteenth-century England. The apple growers of that time performed a year-end wassail bowl ritual as a tribute to the trees. With an ample supply of strong drink containing grated roasted apples, sugars, and eggs, each tree in the orchard received an individual toast, a tip of the cup and a wish for another bountiful crop. The word *wassail* is derived from the Anglo-Saxon *waes hael*, which means "hale to you" or, more literally, "be in good health."

As part of the original toasting practice, the drinking group made loud noises to scare off evil spirits hiding in the trees. The noises became songs, and the overindulged well-wishers then made their way from home to home, continuing to tip the cup, toast each other, and make merriment.

The English wassail bowl custom has become for Americans a punch bowl filled with the popular British pub drink, eggnog. The cry of the original toast, "wassail," is now "cheers," followed by the clinking of glass cups held high.

From whatever source they originally came, American Christmas foods and drinks have distinct tastes and smells that linger from childhood through adulthood. In a world bent upon change, old ways successfully resist the new. Recipes are passed with care from genera-tion to generation, and the good food shared with family and old friends is a major part of today's Christmas tradition. Never should the loving hands and hearts that toil in the kitchen be forgotten, for from them flow the blessed Christmas spirit of the dinner table. ■

The Christmas season truly seems to bring out the best in everyone. Amid all the natural human greed and selfishness, a spirit of generosity and love for others swells as Advent leads us to Christmas Day. From simple dreams in the minds of great individuals have grown far-reaching, sometimes worldwide, organizations that provide seasonal assistance to millions and fill the hearts of children in need with Christmas joy.

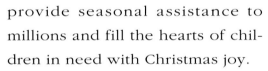

Built on the premise that "every child deserves a little Christmas," Toys for Tots has, in its forty-seven-year existence, delivered toys to more than one hundred million of this nation's less fortunate children.

In 1947, a retired Marine Corps officer, the late Colonel Bill Hendricks, had a desire to brighten the lives of needy children at Christmas. Hendricks's dream began with one of his wife's handmade dolls and his own big heart. He wanted to give the doll to a poor child, but he found there were no agencies organized to distribute toys to needy children. The colonel was moved to start such an organization committed to helping children, and so was born the Marine Corps Reserve's Toys for Tots program.

In that first year, 5,000 toys were collected and distributed in the Los Angeles area. Today, 200 Marine Corps Reserve units across the United States collect approximately 8 million toys each year for children who otherwise would receive nothing.

Practically every community in America either sponsors its own toy drive for children or associates itself with a national effort. Toys for Tots is, by far, the largest nationwide drive dedicated totally to acquiring new toys for children. Many celebrities have joined in the effort, and Walt Disney himself designed the familiar Toys for Tots train logo.

Another project, Secret Santa, began in Parkersburg, West Virginia, and in eleven years has spread to other states. Started by Mary Cunningham as a Jayceette project, it quickly attracted the attention of other communities both in West Virginia and beyond. Secret Santa is a massive volunteer organization in which the volunteers actually Christmas shop for specific children who have written to Santa.

Many charities provide help year-round but capitalize on people's benevolent nature during the spirited Christmas season for their fund-raising. The Salvation Army brings spiritual and practical help to those in need at any time in almost one hundred countries around the world. A significant portion of its funding is gathered at Christmastime, in red kettles to the tune of a hand bell constantly clanging for attention. This uniquely organized group did not originate in America but immigrated from England to New York City in the early 1880s.

Reverend William Booth, a Methodist minister working in London in 1865, began preaching hope and salvation to the city's thieves, prostitutes, gamblers, and drunkards. Many converts were won, but the prim and pious English Christians did not want Booth or his members in their churches or chapels. The innovative and sincere preacher, however, devised a plan of action. He put his converts to work to help save others like themselves. They worked out of their own Christian Mission Centers. Under Booth's leadership, the converts sang in the streets, they paraded and marched, and some even professed their new-found joy as they preached on street corners. Everything in Booth's organization was done in an orderly manner. Soon, the converts began to refer affectionately to their leader as General Booth, and they proudly thought of themselves as the Hallelujah Army.

In the beginning years, Booth permanently placed iron cooking kettles all over London to remind the well-to-do that the less fortunate needed food to cook. The kettles became a symbol of his organization and a constant request for pocket change.

The December month showed such a significant difference in contributions over the other months that the organization decided to increase the effort, but limit it to the month before Christmas. Today, the familiar sounds of the hand bells and the sight of the red kettles are as much a part of Christmas as Santa himself.

In 1876, after more than a decade of growth, the organization formally adopted the name Salvation Army. Meanwhile, the organization was gaining members in the United States and by the mid-1880s was collecting in American towns from coast to coast.

To this day, the Salvation Army continues to operate on the military structure designed by Booth and is a chartered Christian church. Still, its purpose is to express and spread the love of God, always maintaining a practical concern for those in need.

In the autumn of each year,

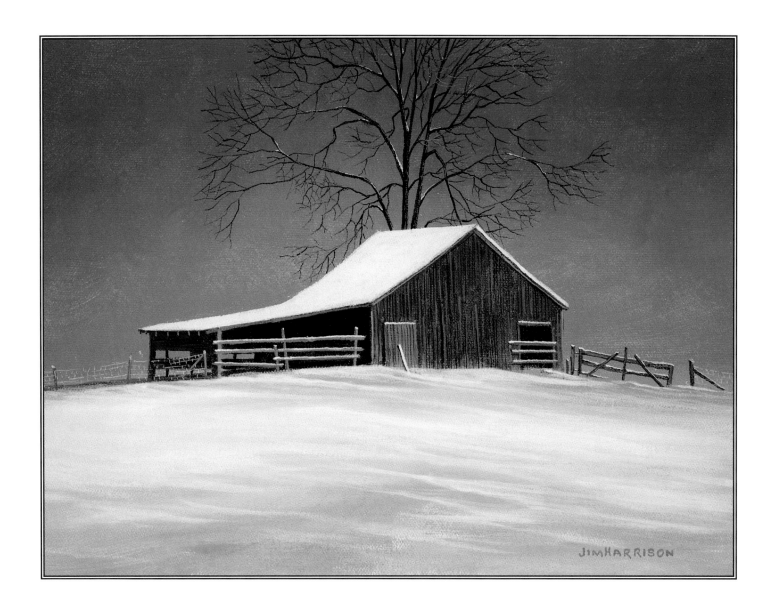

millions of sheets of the American Lung Association's Christmas Seals are mailed to households in every state in America. The annual Christmas Seal campaign is the largest, nonprofit, direct-mail campaign in the country. Christmas Seals, alone, funded the battle to find a cure for the dreaded disease tuberculosis.

The Christmas Seal story actually began in Copenhagen, Denmark, in 1903. A postal clerk, Einar Holboell, got the idea for a decorative Christmas stamp while he was canceling the regular postage stamps on letters. His heartfelt concern for the many tuberculosis sufferers of the time prompted his idea of the sale of stamps for their aid. That year, he had the first Christmas stamps printed and sold 4 million stamps through the post offices of Denmark. The effort generated $18,000 in revenue. Within two years, both Sweden and Norway had joined the effort.

In 1907 in the United States, tuberculosis sanatoriums were springing up around the country. Most were without steady funding and could care for only a few patients at a time. Emily Bissell of Wilmington, Delaware, had developed a particular interest in the small TB hospital in Brandywine. Three hundred dollars was urgently needed to keep its doors open for another year, and funding opportunities had been exhausted. Miss Bissell, the Delaware state secretary of the Red Cross, had read in *The Outlook* an account of the success of the Christmas stamp in Denmark.

She sketched a design, a red cross centered in a half wreath of holly above the words "Merry Christmas." Her associates at the Delaware Red Cross would not agree to finance her stamp plan, but the national office of the organization granted its permission to use its red-cross symbol on the stamps.

Miss Bissell borrowed $40 from friends and had 50,000 seals printed on credit. Efforts to sell them through the post office, however, proved to be futile, so she turned to the good people of Philadelphia for help. She gained a friend in the city's newspaper, *The North American*, which generously promoted the idea daily. President Theodore Roosevelt also endorsed her project. By the time the holiday season was over, $3,000 had been raised.

The American Red Cross was impressed with the results and agreed to sponsor the 1908 campaign. Sales soared to $135,000. By 1920, the National Tuberculosis Association had grown large enough to run the Christmas Seal campaign itself. The bright red, double-barred cross became the emblem of the crusade against TB. The stamps, indeed, did stamp out tuberculosis. Now, annually, the seals continue to be a part of Christmas and help fund the ambitious programs of the American Lung Association.

American charities succeed because we believe in giving to the less fortunate, proving that gladness and generosity go together. The stories of American charities are filled with this desire, and no Christmas season would be complete without their efforts. But beyond these large organizations, and probably exceeding them in scope, are the countless acts of giving among families and individuals throughout the country. In this more personal form, generosity is quite satisfying. Joy and happiness shared are joy and happiness increased. ■

Merry Christmas and Happy New Year are synonymous year-end greetings, extended billions of times to family, friends, and acquaintances around the world during the holiday season. The joint celebration of the birth of Christ and the hailing of the New Year all within the same week seem appropriate. New Year's Day not only marks the beginning of another twelve-month period; it also signals the end of the Christmas season in this country. The actual dates of both holidays have been switched and changed so many times, the two could now be one and the same.

In America today, the essential part of ringing out the old year and bringing in the new is limited to the few minutes before and after midnight on New Year's Eve. At the strike of twelve, the old year falls to the Grim Reaper, Father Time, and the baby New Year is ushered in.

In New York City, an estimated one million people crowd into Times Square and along Broadway for the countdown to end the year. For hours on the eve of the New Year, noise of every description is made until a few seconds before midnight. At that time, all eyes are focused on the glowing, huge ball atop the Times Square building. Millions watch by television as the ball slowly descends during the final, ticking seconds. At exactly twelve o'clock the chimes of old Trinity Church ring out "Auld Lang Syne," and, immediately following, pandemonium again breaks out as the assembled throng cheers in the New Year.

Jim Harrison

This is quite a counterpoint to the nationally televised midnight mass reverently being held only a short distance away in St. Patrick's Cathedral.

Much about the first day of January is ambiguous. Surviving hundreds of years of changes, the secular celebrations and the sacred services still bear a stark contrast. The annual new beginning is a time of hope for the future amid promises of revival and the possibilities for positive change. New Year's resolutions lean toward a better tomorrow, yet memories of the past draw attention to yesterday.

It is no wonder that the first month of the modern calendar is named for the two-faced Roman god, Janus. There are many conflicting stories about January's namesake. Some historians say that Janus derives his name from the Latin word *ianua*, meaning door. He certainly played different roles in the Roman religion, and he was the god who watched over gates and doorways. More significantly, however, Janus was the god of all beginnings. He presided over the first hour of every day and the first day of every month, but the first month of the year was most important to the god.

Janus was depicted visually with two faces looking in opposite directions at the same time. To the left, he viewed the future, and to the right, he peered at the past. Such is the circumstance of a modern-day New Year as both the past and future are celebrated simultaneously.

Dating back to ancient times, the heralding of the first day of the year is one of the oldest festivals observed. January 1 has not always been considered the first day and is, in fact, an unnatural day for that distinction. January 1 has no special place in the sun's cycle and is in no way connected with the winter solstice or equinox. It does seem that the start of a new year should correspond with the beginning of a new season, but January 1 does not.

Centuries ago, various countries had their own ways of marking time and declaring the seasons. Religious beliefs and customs played an important role in influencing the selection of the starting place for the year. As a result, many different calendar positions have been designated as the beginning.

Some ancient people paid homage to the moon and celebrated according to the lunar cycle. The Chinese are moon people who mark the beginning of their calendar year on the day of the second new moon after sunset of the winter solstice.

During the Middle Ages, most Christian countries began the new year on March 25. In 1582, in an

attempt to simplify the marking of time, the Gregorian calendar was adopted by most countries as per a decree from Pope Gregory XIII. Still used today, the Gregorian calendar fixed the first of January as the beginning of the year. In the New World, the Spanish, Portuguese, and French colonies followed the pope's orders. In England and in the English colonies of North America, however, the year continued to begin on March 25 until 1752. It was the strong influence of the Puritans who considered a January 1 celebration to be a blasphemous reference and tribute to the pagan god Janus. The Puritan resistance delayed the English adoption of the Gregorian calendar for almost two hundred years.

The Dutch settlers of the time particularly enjoyed the New Year and made it festive. It was a major holiday in New Nether-land, a time of paying calls and receiving visitors for which much preparation took place. Good food and strong spirits were in abundance, and "calling on folks" was the order of the day.

Even as late as the nineteenth century, it was customary for those who wished to receive guests to list in the local newspapers their names and the hours when their homes would be open. This tradition eventually was undermined by bad manners, gate crashing, and drunkenness, so the open door approach to the social event was abandoned and personal invitations replaced the newspaper announcements.

In the mid-nineteenth century, a purely American custom, Visiting Day, was started and endured for some years. January 1 was selected as an appropriate time for all bachelor gentlemen to visit all maiden ladies. The male callers would begin at midmorning since they had many rounds to make before nightfall. The ladies had silver trays upon which the visitors placed their calling cards, and oftentimes the wise hostess would place a few cards from the previous year upon the tray so as to impress the early callers.

Refreshments included an elaborately decorated cake, eggnog, and a selection of brandies, whiskeys, and wines, but it was considered inappropriate for the men to accept cake when offered. January 2 was reserved for the ladies to visit each other and enjoy the cake with coffee or tea. The ladies' visits provided an ideal opportunity to discuss and compare all the gentlemen callers of the day before.

There was a time in America when gift giving was a part of the New Year's celebration. On the first day of January businessmen had early morning couriers deliver "season's compliments" which were characteristic of the trade of the sender. A butcher sent chickens, a baker delivered bread, and a fisherman gave oysters or shrimp. In return, the delivery boy, even though paid by the gift giver, was treated by each recipient to a glass of wine and a monetary tip.

Queen Elizabeth I of England added a different twist to New Year's gift giving—she declared that it was quite appropriate for ladies to ask for specific items. The queen took this annual opportunity to replenish her wardrobe and her jewel box.

King Henry VIII, who was obligated to give presents of jewelry to a number of ladies, ordered his craftsmen to design and produce a collection of gold lady's lapel pins for his use. So popular were the pins that shortly thereafter, commercial manufacture made them available as expensive New Year's gift items. Men saved money all year for the purchase of pins for their ladies, and those earmarked, year-long savings became known as pin money.

In the United States, the biggest and most festive parties of the year are held on New Year's Eve, while New Year's Day is usually a time of relaxing. Americans are more event oriented than tradition centered, it seems. Most everyone seems to enjoy the televised morning parades, and men especially are glued to the set for the afternoon football games.

Two New Year's events have gained world-wide acclaim. Each year, thousands view in person or via television the Tournament of Roses Parade in Pasadena, California, and the Mummers Parade in Philadelphia, Pennsylvania.

The first Tournament of Roses Parade took place in Pasadena on January 1, 1886. Charles F. Hunt of the Valley Hunt Club is credited with the original idea. Members of the club decorated their carriages with native California flora and paraded through the streets en route to the various athletic events of the day. From that simple beginning, the parade has developed into a pageant unequaled anywhere. Today's athletic event following the parade is one of the top college football games of the season, the Rose Bowl.

The Rose Bowl Queen leads the parade, a procession filled with unbelievable, creative floats covered with thousands of roses and other exotic flowers. Each year, a different theme is selected, and the float participants must all agree to carry out that idea in flowers. School bands from all over the nation are invited to march and are interspersed among the floats, but the focus remains clearly on the abundant native California flora.

In Philadelphia, viewers are treated to a ten-hour spectacle, the Mummers Parade. This strange custom came to America from Sweden, but it actually originated in England. Delaware River immigrants welcomed the New Year by dressing in outlandish outfits and parading around town in groups, creating noise and fun for their neighbors and fellow townspeople.

In the medieval European tradition, mummers disguised themselves and, thus uninhibited, traveled afoot performing an informal, comical play to entertain their neighbors. Once recognized, the actors were expected to remove their disguises and receive a handout of money, food, or strong drink from their audience.

The parade is now much more formal and extends over a four-mile route through the downtown of the historic city. No women are allowed to participate; however, some of the men dress and act the part of women in this colorful event. King Momus, who is elaborately dressed in satin, linen, and sequins, is the featured character, and he is attended by mummers disguised as wild animals, outlaws, and a variety of other oddfellows. String bands provide traditional banjo rhythms, and marching groups add a sense of order to this unique presentation.

New Year's Day is a national, legal holiday, and is a welcomed vacation respite before tackling the chores of the ensuing 364 days. The twelve-month cycle then begins anew, as it has for hundreds of years, with revived enthusiasm, spirit, and hope.

Epilogue

So be it. With or without the snow, we do have our own true American Christmas. Our present holiday ways have been melted together from many sources—with a few new ideas thrown in, of course. Without a doubt, the annual December birthday for Jesus is by far America's favorite and most celebrated day of the year.

Christmas may be a festive time for children, but it is also the one occasion of the year when adults would like to revert to childhood and enjoy, again, the days of their youth. Try as we may, the futile attempt to return to the past is usually no more than a fleeting moment of excitement as we recall faded excerpts from the carefree days of growing up. It just doesn't work that way. But I've come close, and I've just had a ball for the past year.

Researching the material for this book has allowed me to enjoy nearly two thousand Christmases. For the last twelve months, I've gone to bed each night to the sound of sleigh bells and awakened every morning to snow-covered landscapes, if only in my mind.

In this fast-paced, nuclear age, astronauts now walk on the moon; scientists talk of trips through the heavens to other planets and other worlds. Hardly one barrier is broken before the next challenge is before us. We live with the constant pressure for stronger rockets, faster computers, and quicker hamburgers.

Let's never allow this progress-driven, goal-oriented mentality to interfere with our basic Christmas beliefs and the traditions so loved by our forefathers and mothers.

The task is difficult, for many of our current Christmas ways came to us through country folks, and it seems that most often we associate the good old days with a rural, agricultural setting. But life and the social patterns in our country have drastically changed over the last hundred years. The slow, calm lifestyle of a simple farmer of yesteryear no longer exists. Today is the age of speed, sophistication, and advanced technology. These current trends have a tendency to put greater distance between us and our beloved past.

Still, old ways don't die easily. The present young generation has a keen interest in the ways of their ancestors. For these maturing youngsters, the attraction well may be a perception of simpler, easier, happier times. Their search for such times is not all bad, and is quite refreshing when contrasted with the fast-paced, materialistic mood so prevalent in today's world.

Christmas is a time for bridging the distance between the past and the present. With the earth spinning at about a thousand miles an hour, Christmas offers us a season to slow our pace and to renew our spirits. Christmas is the one moment of the year when all of us need to be reminded that this old world cannot successfully continue without faith, hope, and charity.

❄ ❄ ❄

Merry Christmas to all and a Happy New Year,

Jim Harrison